MW01055414

Road to Revolution

Francis Downey

PICTURE CREDITS

Cover, pages 10–11, 12 (top), 13, 25 (top right and bottom left), 26–27, 28–29 (top), 31 (top), 35-a, 35-c, 35-e © Bettman/CORBIS; title page © Kevin Fleming/CORBIS; pages 2–3, 8, 9, 12 (bottom), 14 (left and center), 15 (left and right), 20, 21, 22 (bottom), 23 (right), 25 (bottom right), 27, 29 (top right), 30 (top), 31 (center), 34-c, 34-e, 35-b, 35-d © The Granger Collection, New York; pages 4–5, 25 (top left), 34-a illustrations by Paul Mirocha; pages 6–7, 31 (bottom), 34-d © Craig Miller/www.secondalbany.org; pages 6–7 (background) © Royalty-Free/CORBIS; pages 10, 30 (bottom) © Time Life Pictures/Getty Images; page 14 (right) © Massachusetts Historical Society, Boston, MA, USA/The Bridgeman Art Library; page 15 (center) © Joseph Sohm, Visions of America/CORBIS; pages 16–17 © Dennis Hallinan/Alamy; page 18 © UnumProvident Corporation; pages 19 (left), 36 © Concord Museum, Concord, MA; page 19 (right) © Rick Friedman/CORBIS; pages 22–23 (top center), 35-e © Freelance Photography Guild/CORBIS; pages 28–29 (inset) © Northampton Museums, Northampton Borough Council; page 29 (bottom left) courtesy The Bostonian Society/Old State House Museum; page 32 © National Parks Service; page 33 (left) *Fight for Freedom* by Daniel Rosen, © 2003 National Geographic Society, photos (inset) © National Portrait Gallery, Smithsonian Institution/Art Resource, NY, (background) © CORBIS, (center) *The Declaration of Independence* by Judith Lloyd Yero, © 2004 National Geographic Society, photos (inset) © Independence National Historic Park Collection, (top background) © Rubberball Productions/Getty Images, (bottom background) © Joseph Sohm/CORBIS, (right) *Colonial Life* by Barbara Burt, © 2002 National Geographic Society, photo © The Granger Collection, New York; page 34 © Barry Winiker/Index Stock Imagery.

Produced through the worldwide resources of the National Geographic Society, John M. Fahey, Jr., President and Chief Executive Officer; Gilbert M. Grosvenor, Chairman of the Board; Nina D. Hoffman, Executive Vice President and President, Books and Education Publishing Group.

PREPARED BY NATIONAL GEOGRAPHIC SCHOOL PUBLISHING

Ericka Markman, Senior Vice President and President, Children's Books and Education Publishing Group; Steve Mico, Senior Vice President, Editorial Director, Publisher; Francis Downey, Executive Editor; Richard Easby, Editorial Manager; Anne Stone, Lori Dibble Collins, Editors; Bea Jackson, Director of Layout and Design; Jim Hiscott, Design Manager; Cynthia Olson, Art Director; Margaret Sidlosky, Illustrations Director; Matt Wascavage, Manager of Publishing Services; Sean Philpotts, Jane Ponton, Production Managers; Ted Tucker, Production Specialist.

MANUFACTURING AND QUALITY CONTROL

Christopher A. Liedel, Chief Financial Officer; Phillip L. Schlosser, Director; Clifton M. Brown III, Manager

CONSULTANT AND REVIEWER

J.M. Opal, Colby College

BOOK DESIGN/PHOTO RESEARCH

Steve Curtis Design, Inc.

◀ English soldiers march during the Revolutionary War.

Contents

Published by the National Geographic Society
1145 17th Street N.W.
Washington, D.C. 20036-4688

ISBN: 0-7922-5452-X

2010 2009 2008 2007 2006
1 2 3 4 5 6 7 8 9 10 11 12 13 14 15

Printed in Canada.

The Thirteen Colonies

Colonies

Long ago, the United States was different than it is today. It was not even a country. Instead, it was 13 **colonies**. A colony is a place ruled by another country. England **governed**, or ruled, all 13 colonies. The first English colony was settled in 1607.

People in each colony did not think that they had much in common with the other colonies. They did not think they were Americans. The people of New York thought of themselves as New Yorkers. And the people of Virginia called themselves Virginians.

colony – a place ruled by another country

govern – to rule

▶ **England had 13 colonies in what is now the United States.**

4

England

New Hampshire

Massachusetts

New York

Rhode Island

Connecticut

Pennsylvania

New Jersey

Delaware

Maryland

Virginia

North Carolina

South Carolina

Georgia

Atlantic

Ocean

Big Idea
New laws and taxes caused the American Revolution.

Set Purpose
Learn what events led to the American Revolution.

Fighting New

▼ People reenact a battle from the American Revolution.

Questions You Will Explore

What events led to the American Revolution?

How did the American Revolution begin?

for a Nation

In 1776, **colonists** living in the 13 colonies decided to go to war. They went to war against England because they wanted to be free. They wanted to rule themselves.

A war to replace one government with another is called a **revolution**. The war between England and the 13 colonies is called the American Revolution.

Deciding to go to war was hard. It took a long time for the colonists to decide to start the American Revolution.

colonist – a person who lives in a colony

revolution – a war to replace one government with another government

▲ Native Americans help the French fight a war against the English.

French and Indian War

Troubles with England started in 1763. That is when a war between England and France ended. We often call this war the French and Indian War. England won the war. At first, the colonists were happy. But that did not last. Why?

▲ **English lawmakers talk about the colonies.**

New Laws

England passed new laws. The colonists did not like the new laws. For example, one law kept the colonists from moving west of the colonies. Native Americans lived in much of that area. England was afraid the colonists would start a war with the Native Americans. England could not afford a new war.

▲ Colonists chase tax
collectors out of town.

New Taxes

England also passed new **taxes.** One tax made the
colonists buy stamps and put them on many paper
goods. Stamps had to be placed on contracts,
calendars, newspapers, and even playing cards.
The tax made paper goods more expensive.

Many colonists fought the stamp tax. They did not
buy the stamps. Instead, they ran the stamp sellers
out of their towns. They **protested** the tax.

tax – money collected by the government to pay for services

protest – to speak out against

10

▲ Colonists dump crates of tea into Boston Harbor.

Trouble in Boston

The protests worked. England ended the stamp tax. But the troubles did not end. England passed more laws and taxes.

In 1773, England passed a tax on tea. Colonists in several colonies protested against the tax. Some colonists held tea parties. They dressed as Indians and then boarded ships carrying tea. They tossed crates of tea into the ocean. The most famous of these protests is known as the Boston Tea Party.

▲ Ships loaded with English soldiers sail into Boston Harbor.

Loss of Freedom

After the Boston Tea Party, England punished the people of Boston. England closed Boston Harbor. Ships could not go in or out. Town meetings were outlawed. The colonists felt they were losing their freedom.

Colonists from 12 of the colonies held a meeting in Philadelphia. They wanted to stay loyal to the King of England. But they decided to send a letter to him. They asked him to end the tax on tea.

▲ Colonists meet in Philadelphia.

▲ Redcoats and minutemen
fight in Lexington,
Massachusetts.

Moving Toward War

In Massachusetts, some colonists started training
for war. These colonists claimed they could fight
on a minute's notice. They were called **minutemen**.

Some minutemen hid weapons in Concord.
It is a town near Boston. But the English soldiers,
or **redcoats**, soon learned about the weapons. On
the night of April 18, 1775, the redcoats marched
to Concord. The next day they fought battles at
Lexington and Concord.

minuteman – a colonial soldier who could fight on a minute's notice

redcoat – an English soldier who wore a red uniform

American Revolution Time Line

1763	1765	1773

French and Indian War Ends

England Enacts Stamp Tax

England Taxes Tea

▲ Native Americans meet with French soldiers.

▲ Tax stamp

▲ Tea leaves recovered from Boston Harbor

Fighting the War

Soon the colonists and redcoats were fighting more battles. The colonists won many of the first battles. In July 1776, the colonists stated that they wanted to be free of English rule. Fighting spread throughout the 13 colonies.

In 1778, France joined with the Americans to fight against England. France used its powerful navy to block English ships from coming to America.

1775	1776	1781

American Revolution Begins

Colonists Declare Independence

American Revolution Ends

▲ Battle of Concord

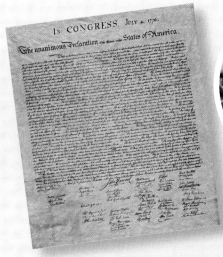

▲ Declaration of Independence

▲ England surrenders at Yorktown.

Surrender

The American Revolution finally ended in 1781. After losing a battle at Yorktown, Virginia, an English general surrendered. The 13 colonies had won the war against England.

As the English surrendered, a band played a song that was popular at the time. It was called "The World Turned Upside Down." The war had changed the entire world. A new nation was created.

Stop and Think!

What events led to the American Revolution?

2 Take a Closer Look

Recap
Explain how the American
Revolution started.

Set Purpose
Learn about how the
Americans knew the
redcoats were marching
toward Lexington
and Concord.

MEET PAUL REVERE

Paul Revere was born in Boston, Massachusetts, in 1735. He was a **silversmith**. He created and sold objects made out of silver. For example, he made teapots and silver trays.

Paul Revere was also a **patriot**. He wanted the colonies to be free from English rule. He was willing to risk his life to fight against England. He did just that on his midnight ride to Lexington.

....

silversmith – a person who makes things out of silver

patriot – a colonist who wanted independence

▲ This statue of Paul Revere stands in Boston, Massachusetts.

17

Redcoats

By April 1775, Boston was not safe for patriots. In fact, most of them had left town. Paul Revere stayed behind. He stayed to learn what the redcoats were planning.

The redcoats were watching, too. They had their eyes on Revere. They knew that he had been meeting with other patriots outside of town. They also knew that he had been telling the patriots what the redcoats were doing.

▶ **Patriots hung two lamps like this one in the tower of the Old North Church.**

▼ **Paul Revere crosses Boston Harbor as a British ship keeps a close watch.**

▶ Tower of the Old North Church

Lamps hung here

Secret Code

Revere worried that the redcoats would catch him and other patriots. He and his friends came up with a secret code. The code would warn the patriots what the redcoats were doing.

Revere asked friends to put lamps in the tower of the Old North Church. The lamps would tell which way the redcoats were moving. One lamp meant the redcoats were leaving Boston on the south road. Two lamps meant they were leaving Boston in boats.

The Redcoats Are Coming!

On April 18, Revere's plan went into action. The redcoats were on the move. They were moving toward Concord to capture weapons that had been hidden there. Revere and another rider mounted horses. They rode toward Lexington and Concord.

▼ Paul Revere looks back at the lights in the Old North Church.

Lamps in Old North Church

▲ Paul Revere warns colonists
that the redcoats are coming.

The Midnight Ride

It was midnight when Revere reached
Lexington. It was late, but he was hours ahead
of the redcoats. He warned two patriot leaders
to get out of town. They were in danger of
being captured by the redcoats.

Revere rested for a short time. Then he and
two other riders rode toward Concord. They
wanted to warn the colonists that the redcoats
were coming. They rode straight into a trap.

A Close Call

English soldiers on horseback closed in around the men. Revere was captured and questioned. He told the redcoats that the minutemen were gathering. He told the redcoats that their lives were in danger.

When the redcoats heard nearby shots, they knew that Revere was telling the truth. They took Revere's horse and let him go. Revere returned to Lexington on foot.

▶ Redcoats chase
Paul Revere.

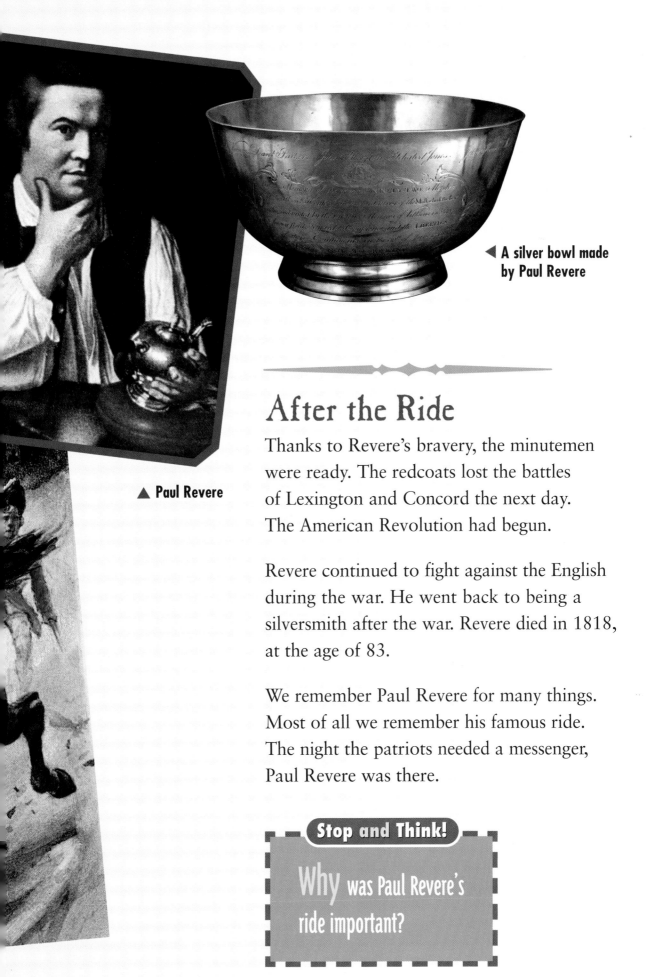

▲ Paul Revere

◀ A silver bowl made by Paul Revere

After the Ride

Thanks to Revere's bravery, the minutemen were ready. The redcoats lost the battles of Lexington and Concord the next day. The American Revolution had begun.

Revere continued to fight against the English during the war. He went back to being a silversmith after the war. Revere died in 1818, at the age of 83.

We remember Paul Revere for many things. Most of all we remember his famous ride. The night the patriots needed a messenger, Paul Revere was there.

Stop and Think!

Why was Paul Revere's ride important?

Recap
Tell why Paul Revere's ride was important to the American Revolution.

Set Purpose
Now read about other events that led to the American Revolution.

CONNECT WHAT YOU HAVE LEARNED

Road to Revolution

The United States did not become a country until 1781. Before then, many of the people lived in colonies ruled by England. The colonists fought a war to win their independence.

Here are some ideas that you learned about the events that led to the American Revolution.

- The United States started out as 13 colonies ruled by England.
- England passed laws and taxes the colonists did not like.
- The American Revolution started with battles at Lexington and Concord.
- A new country was born when the American Revolution ended in 1781.

Check What You Have Learned

Why is the American Revolution important?

▲ This map shows the 13 English colonies.

▲ Colonists protest the tax on tea.

▲ Redcoats fight the minutemen in Lexington.

▲ Colonists meet to plan a new government.

Voting for War

The Battle of Lexington and Concord took place in April 1775. England and the colonies were at war after the battle. Yet many Americans were not ready to break from England. Some wanted peace.

American leaders talked about war for more than a year. Finally, in the summer of 1776, colonial leaders passed the Declaration of Independence. This paper told England that America wanted to rule itself.

First draft of
the Declaration
of Independence

American leaders present
the Declaration of
Independence in 1776.

▲ The Boston Tea Party

The Shoemaker's Tale

The Boston Tea Party is one of the most famous events in United States history. Yet no one knows most of the people who took part in it. We do know about George Robert Twelves Hewes. He was a shoemaker.

On December 16, 1773, Hewes and others dressed as Indians. They quickly boarded three ships in Boston Harbor. Using axes, they broke open crates of tea and tossed the tea overboard. Later, Hewes fought in the American Revolution.

▲ **George Washington accepts command of the United States Army.**

Commander in Chief

George Washington was a patriot. He thought English rule was too harsh. He was willing to go to war to gain independence.

In 1775, Washington was elected the first commander in chief of the Continental Army. He quickly decided that he would lead the army without pay.

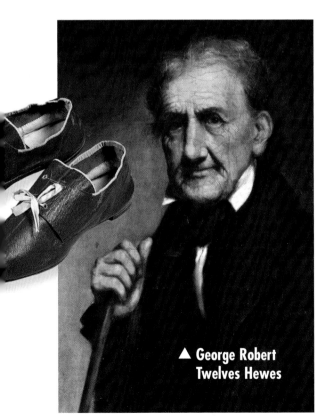

▲ **George Robert Twelves Hewes**

Many kinds of words are used in this book. Here you will learn about contractions. You will also learn about compound words.

Contractions

A contraction is a shortened form of two words. It is made by leaving out some letters and adding an apostrophe. What contractions do you already know?

that is = that's

That's why the patriots fought for freedom.

did not = didn't

The colonists **didn't** buy the stamps.

Compound Words

A compound word is made by joining two shorter words. You can often figure out what a compound word means by knowing what the two shorter words mean.

shoe + maker = shoemaker

Long ago, people bought shoes from a **shoemaker.**

red + coat = redcoat

British soldiers were called **redcoats.**

minute + men = minutemen

The **minutemen** were ready to fight on a minute's notice.

Research and Write

Write About the American Revolution

Research both sides of the war. Why did England want to keep its colonies? Why did Americans want their freedom? Which people were important to the fight for independence?

Research
Collect books and reference materials, or go online.

Read and Take Notes
As you read, take notes and draw pictures.

Write
Pick one side of the American Revolution. Write about why people on that side thought they were correct.

Read and Compare

Read More About the American Revolution

Find and read other books about America before and during the American Revolution. As you read, think about these questions.

- What was America fighting for?
- How was life different than life today?
- Why was the Declaration of Independence important?

Books to Read

▲ Read how the colonies won their independence from England.

▲ Explore the story of the Declaration and its meaning today.

▲ Learn more about the adventures of a boy in colonial America.

Glossary

colonist (page 7)
A person who lives in a colony
In 1776, colonists living in the 13 colonies decided to go to war.

colony (page 4)
A place ruled by another country
England had 13 colonies in what is now the United States.

govern (page 4)
To rule
England governed all 13 colonies.

minuteman (page 13)
A colonial soldier who could fight on a minute's notice
Some minutemen hid weapons in Concord.

patriot (page 17)
A colonist who wanted independence
Paul Revere was a patriot.

protest (page 10)
To speak out against
Colonists protested the tax on tea.

redcoat (page 13)
An English soldier who wore a red uniform
Soon the redcoats and the colonists were fighting more battles.

revolution (page 7)
A war to replace one government with another government
The war between England and its 13 colonies is called the American Revolution.

silversmith (page 17)
A person who makes things out of silver
Paul Revere was a silversmith.

tax (page 10)
Money collected by the government to pay for services
England passed a tax on tea.

35

Index